Bright Lights in A Dim Universe: *Expanded Edition*

Written by: E. L. Barnes

Copyright © 2023 E. L. Barnes
All rights reserved.
ISBN:
979-8-3975-3634-9

Dedication:

To that noob (I call a friend), my bro for life, the warrior at heart, my sassy life coach, and that guy who stayed up till one a.m. helping me finish my final exam. I love you guys. Thanks for the laughter, memories, inside jokes, and inspiration.

All to You, my Blessed Savior. Thank You for being the Light to my darkness.

I surrender all.

~ 2 Timothy 1:7 ~

Acknowledgement:

There are so many people to give thanks to and *for* that this section could take easily take up 25% or more of this book so I'll just say this:

Thank you to my Mom, Dad, and brother for pushing me forward toward greatness, for pulling me to my feet whenever I feel cast down, and for encouraging me when the only voice I hear is my own, telling me I *can't*. Of course, *I* can't. Not on my own. And that's why I say:

Thank you, thank you, thank you all. You are true bright lights.

A Quick Note to Readers:

You might have noticed that there is a lot of blank space in this book. That is intentional. More importantly, that space is for you. (Yes, you.) It's a space to dump scattered thoughts, ideas, inspirations, doodles, etc. Whenever I read something, whether it be new or familiar, I'm amazed at the connections I can make to my own life, the things I learn about myself and others, and most especially, the things I discover about the existence of a living, loving God. So please, use the blank space as *your* blank space...and fill it with the breathings of your heart.

Much love,

E. L. Barnes

Table of Contents

Part I *9*

    I Am 10

    Confidence 11

    Lilies Fade 12

    A New Day 13

    Your Smile 14

    Broken Glass 15

    Summer at the RV 16

    Lesson of the Waves 17

Part II *18*

    To You from Me 19

    Fact or Fiction 20

    A Warped Remembrance 21

    People Ask Me 22

    In My Bones 24

    Ode to Hand Sanitizer 26

    I h8te it when… 27

    Restlessness 29

    Scars & Redemption 30

Nursery Rhyme 33

The Greatest Trial 34

#brosforlife 35

For A Little Bit 37

A Fond Remembrance 38

Ode to a Rose 40

Ode to Self-Doubt 41

A week in the life of a 23-year-old college student – 42

ADC 48

Memos 49

Houseguests 50

Part III *63*

The Scary Thing 64

#2020 65

Vulnerable 66

Heart Cry 67

Count Your Blessings 68

Life in Living Colors 71

Up in Flames 72

Disguise 73

Something New 74

Dangerous Melody 75

Bright Lights in A Dim Universe: ***Expanded Edition***

Does it Ever Occur to You? 76

dancing barefoot in the grass with You 77

The Recipe of a Faithful Servant 78

That's the Tea 79

Melt Away 80

Storm 81

Ode to Evie 82

A Love Letter to Close 83

E. L. Barnes

Part I

I Am

I am innocence in its purest form,
The simplicity of life.
I am the essence of creativity,
Imagination and excitement,
Full of bright-eyed wonder.
I am the explorer of new worlds,
Anxiously waiting for whatever
my future holds.
I am the one, who connects distant
memories,
For those who have forgotten.
I am the everlasting glow of
Youth,

I am a child.

E. L. Barnes

Confidence

Confidence is a loyal, supporting friend.
She wakes you up and sprinkles you with compliments,
sending you on your way, to embrace the day.
She knows your accomplishments
and talents; your number one fan.

Confidence is a steaming cup of hot chocolate,
sending warm waves all throughout the
inner workings of your heart.
It reaches your face and covers you with a satisfied grin.

Confidence is a shining gold key
wrapped in self-expression,
unlocking your true potential,
exposing your human self,
for the whole world to see.

Lilies Fade

Bobbing lilies sit,
Awaiting a single prick;
A girl's homemade crown.

E. L. Barnes

A New Day

It's the beginning of a new day,
The Sun smiles.
With a brilliant burst of Summer's orange,
She kisses the thirsty flowers.
It's time for afternoon tea,
The Sun dances.
With a jolt of excitement,
She glides over a shining afternoon.
The day is coming to an end,
The Sun yawns.
With an exhausted exhale of hot air,
She sighs over a sagging sunset.
It's time to part with the day,
The Sun cries.
With a glum countenance,
She hides in an ever-darkening sky.

Your Smile

Walking to the back,
of the welcoming house I've spent countless summers in,
And on the old, familiar, leather couch of the television room,
Is no one.
And in my heart creeps the sudden gloom.
I'm then reminded of the sweetest times;
Times before miles divided us.
Days of laughing around the kitchen table,
Eating delicious homemade food,
Until due to sickness you were unable.
Your smile;
Your slow,
Smooth,
Toothy smile,
Was always the cheerful song that lifted my mood.
Now it's gone.
I only have pictures to hold close,
To remember your kind heart.
How I wished I could have been there,
How I wished we hadn't ever been apart.
It's been a year and I still think of you,
When I clean,
When I sing.
I see you standing in the back row,
Laughing with the One, True King.
And it's the most beautiful thing I've ever seen.

E. L. Barnes

Broken Glass

It hurts so bad,
Walking on this broken glass.
A wave, a smile,
And the tears come rushing back.
I've been shattered.

The day's turn to gray,
Will things ever be okay?
I'm in between,
A restless and a broken sleep.

My heart's in tatters.

Summer at the RV

The Sun wraps me in its arms,
Massaging my shoulders as I sleep.
As I dream my skin burns,
Laying a series of fire-kissed thorns,
Across my back.
I roll over to seek relief,
From the Fiery Culprit of my grief,
Unaware that by turning over,
I give King Solar another poker.
It's only a matter of time,
Before my mother chimes:
"Pack your things and find your fins,
It's time for us to go."
I love the beach,
I really do.
It's hard to bid the shore adieu.
But as for the Sun,
That sly orange fox,
I wish I had at least brought some sunblock.
Perhaps even some flip-flops?

E. L. Barnes

Lesson of the Waves

Over, under, down, and back,
I see the waves
Foam and crack.

One moment close,
Another apart,
How can they be content thus far?

A wave is born,
And then it dies.
Its beauty and power forever capsized.

A wave's but a breath,
A soggy gasp,
On the turbulent path that leads to death.

Bright Lights in A Dim Universe: ***Expanded Edition***

Part II

E. L. Barnes

To You from Me

Your ridges of pearls, sweeping across
The alabaster neckline of your beaded
periwinkle dress.
The timid blue in between your ornamental
beauty,
Matched to the speckled hue of the robin's egg.
And those little flecks of geology,
Herald the diorite's arrival to the scene.
Not as subtle as the cherry wood,
With its deep russets and bright reds,
And less tranquil than the grazing abrasions
Of the champagne-drenched sand.
Yet still more magnificent that the dirt
Beneath my feet.
More magnificent than the debris
Marring the recesses of my cluttered colorless
heart.

Fact or Fiction

The **raw**, beating heart,
A coffin or basket-case:
Can't **hold** everything.

E. L. Barnes

A Warped Remembrance

I remember one day in August, it was a hundred-and-
two degrees out. You could cook an egg on the sidewalk.
I was eight years old.
I told Father I was hot. It was too hot to play with my
friends. I started to cry. I remember he picked me up
and took me out to the backyard and told me to run
around in the grass. Then, he took out his pocket
knife and grabbed the hose. He poked holes in the
hose while I ran around and then turned on the water.
He sprayed it at me and suddenly I wasn't hot.
I was cold. He made it cold for me.

~

I remember one day. It was in September.
The leaves had just started to change.
I was twelve.
I was out with my pals having a grand old time
chucking stones at a bird's nest in the big oak tree
out front when Father came home. He saw me.
He slammed the door of his truck. He grabbed
me by my collar with one hand and took off his
belt with the other. Then he spanked me.
He spanked me in front of my friends until
I cried. And suddenly it was cold.
I was cold. He made it cold for me.

People Ask Me

"If our hearts condemn us, we know that God is greater than our hearts, and He Knows everything.
~ 1 John 3:20

Some people ask me:
"How is it being bipolar? It must be hell."
It's not.

Hell would imply a fiery furnace of eternal despair,
Pain and sorrow and the gnashing of teeth,
Would imply knowing that I'm in a bad place,
And actually caring about finding myself there.

Bipolar definitely isn't Heaven.
Gilded angels, choirs singing, streets of gold-
No.

It's not Heaven.

So what is it, then? Purgatory?
No, Purgatory requires presence.
I dwell in absence.

I'm not suffering.
I'm not.
I feel nothing.

Bipolar isn't fire.
Not ice either.
It's neither hot nor cold.

It's *screaming underwater.*
You hear the gurgles,
But not the emotion.
Muffled detachment.

It's lukewarm.
Tepid bathwater.
.
.
.

"How is it being you? Must be nice."

In My Bones

To my Mother,
The dreamer, the lover, the fighter.

It starts as a twinge, an unpleasant ache,
You pop a few Advil in your palm to take.
Too much laundry, husband's a pest?
You give it your best half-baked guess.

It goes away for a while...

Sweet relief.
Things go back to normal for a couple of weeks.
Then one fateful night,
When you think you can do it all...

911, an ambulance, an x-ray.
"Just give me something to take this freaking pain away."
Waiting
.
.
.
for
.
.
.
hours,
Your friends bringing flowers,
"You've broken your hip, ma'am,
You have bone cancer too,"

E. L. Barnes

Now the only question is:
What will you do?

Ode to Hand Sanitizer

You ooze into my cuts and the crevices of
My hands.
Your slimy green tentacles latch on the surface
of
My skin.
Gone are the germs ruling my life.
Gone is the fear of the unknown.
Gone are the voices colored by my OCD
whispering,
"You could die. You. Could. Die."
With one pump, I'm set free.
With one pump, I can breathe.
99.9% gone? I'll take those odds.

COVID ain't got nothing on me.

E. L. Barnes

I h8te it when...

*To that person with a bad case of text
anxiety and unrequited love.*

Hi!
5:02 pm

Heyy
6:00 pm
How's it going?
6:05 pm

I'm just chillin ;P
6:49 pm
Hbu?
7:15 pm

Hello??
8:06 pm
I h8 it when I have to text u first.
Do u realize how hard it is for me to do that?
8:10 pm
First, I have to think of a legitimate excuse.
(...)
Did u finish that hmwrk assignment?
Do u have the notes from last class?
Are u working on that essay yet?
(...)
It's either that or come up with something witty
and last I checked I am NOT a witty human
being.

I'm barely a functioning human being. #butsrsly
(...)
After I finally figure out what to say,
then there's the all-important question
Do I or do I not include emojis?
If so, what kinds? Should I do a ;P or just a ;)?
Is one flirtier than the other???
(Omgosh just kill me now...)
What about a thumbs-up, or am I just
friend-zoning myself?
#frickmylife
(...)
By this time, it's been 30 mins.
I send the text and wait.
And wait,
And waaaaaaaaaait.
(gross my palms are sweat-ING)
It takes nearly three HOURS for you to respond
after what felt like an eternity for me to get up
the courage to send a freaking text!!
I start to ask myself
Does he think I'm bothering him?
Is this his "subtle" way of telling me to
back off?
Is he rejecting me?
...why is he rejecting me?
8:21 pm

                                              (...)
                                              (...)
                                             read

E. L. Barnes

Restlessness

The pools of green,
Whistle in the night.
They rustle in the summer,
Never once stopping,
For breath.

Scars & Redemption

I have these scars on the sides
Of my arms.
Gathered over years and years.
To me, they've just appeared
They bubble and blister and crack and scream
Tearing off band-aids and a number
Of things I've tried to ply over
The pain that was created by
"Just a dream."

But I can attest,
My scars are not part of some
Fantastical dream,
I honestly wish they were,
At least then my arms would
Be clean.

But these broken seams sting too much
Too ignore,
These torn up, ripped out
Stitches burn too hot to be pushed
Aside anymore.

No--
I cannot stay silent.
Because these things on my arm, that
You call, I call, ugly and obscene
Are the reasons why I am now called
Redeemed.

See, I'm not the only one with scars.
Mine are on my arms
His were on His hands and feet
On the temples of His glorious
Head, and beneath His arm
Pierced in His side.

Rejected by the entire world
Compared to His life,
His pain
We have something in common then,
Him and I.

Yet when He died, I survived.
He gave His life so I could
Have the chance to thrive.
And like Him, even when
I find myself in the
Valley of the grave, I
Will rise.

I have these scar,
These beautiful scars.
Gathered over years and years.
I'm not sure when they got
There.

Some days, it's like they've just appeared.
But I will not be silent.
I will not be cast down.
For I once was lost, but now I'm

Found.

I once was bound up, cut
Down, gagged and shackled and chained.
I was once shut out, stomped
On, tossed away, forgotten,
Left to stitch up these
Wounds all on my own.

But thanks to Him and His beautiful scars,
I have been set free.
By those scars, I am healed.
And by those same scars,
I have,
I am,
And I will always be

Redeemed.

E. L. Barnes

Nursery Rhyme

I unpacked a little nesting doll,
With eyes of cornflower blue,
From a trunk with match-lit marks,
Across the top.
And the eerie stillness in her eyes,
Reverberated through the attic of my heart.

The Greatest Trial

You push my head down to the ground...
When all I want is a pillow to
Block you out.
I flip and turn and toss around,
Throwing my sheets in a raging fit,
When all I want is to stop
The sound...of your voice.
But you're in my head,
You're in my skin,
You're the breath I breathe out
And the breath I breathe in.
You're closer than a friend
And crueler than the cruelest side of
A two-edged knife.
You're the greatest trial of my life.

E. L. Barnes

#brosforlife

*To Malcolm. (Thanks for reaching out
when I still didn't like you.)*

Do you remember that first day? Auditions,
Callbacks, the Scottish Play?
I heard about you and didn't like you---
I was
intimidated.
But I figured, playing brothers,
We should try to be friends; be professionals if
nothing else.
And so it began: scansion and Shakespeare.
Kicking duct tape blocks across MWAT.
7-minute workouts...Dying during said 7-
minute workouts.
Being manly. (Which were totally successful
at, by the way.)
Fleeing to Europe to escape a murderous
Dictator.
#brosforlife.

Oh, and do you remember what came next?
There are so many moments, but here are my favorites:
Feetleese (kick off your Sunday sheese).
Acting II.
The Shape of Things.
Aussie vs. Brit.
Festival.
One rum and Pepsi mistake.

Several episodes of Married at First Sight---
imaginary dollars.
#brosforlife.

And do you remember where we are now?
Shirley. Temples.
With two cherries (at least).
Shirley temples with Alex freaking Harding.
Shirley Temples during quarantine.
Shirley Temples at Side Bar.
Salads and slurps and girl talk and punting me like a football.
Applebee's fries and blackberry lemonade and super buttery popcorn and watching plays.
These are the marks of a bro.
#brosforlife.

E. L. Barnes

For A Little Bit

He leaves the room and her heart breaks a little bit.
He and she knew each other once, just a little bit.

Straightening his tie and kissing his neck,
He used to love her touch, just a little bit.

The obligatory wedding date never felt forced.
They made a handsome couple, for a little bit.

Theirs was a story written in the stars,
At least that's what everyone use to say, for a little bit.

One night of regret,
And a corner of my soul rips, more than a little bit.

A Fond Remembrance

My fingers tickle across the black and white keys,
Mimicking the titillating nature of tinkling glass,
And the swathy highs of the gray skies,
Blow my heap of baby rose petals,
Into the mouth of a dog,
Who frolics in the midst of it all with a baby.

A fairy's baby,
Jingling a set of gnarled up keys,
Taunts the little black and white dog,
As they dance in an orb of glass.
Nipping and biting and snapping at petals,
The duo revels in the painting of the ombre skies.

The melancholy skies
Coddle and cuddle and coo at the sprite's baby,
Making for him a crown of the crispest flower petals,
As a bribe for a set of keys,
To leave behind an arc of broken glass,
Under the protection of one loyal dog.

The joyous bark of a dog,
The potential rain of the weepy skies,
And filmy shards of shattered glass,
All make for white noise to a baby,
Add some keys,

To the mobile and finish with a sprinkling of petals.

The whitest snowflakes preserved in ivory rose petals,
That become lunch for the terrier dog,
Not unlike the bronze and brazen keys,
That signal lighting form the charged skies,
Attuned to the crying of the fairy baby,
Which is as fragile as freshly blown glass.

I see myself in mutilated glass,
The ripped and worn pasty petals,
And wailing elf-baby.
I see myself in the exuberance of a dog,
Even as my heart sobs like the tender-blue skies.
My emotions jingling and jangling like out-of-tune piano keys.

The glass tear slips through the tears of the blush pink petals,
Bouncing off the dog before delighting a squealing baby,
Scattering the keys and restoring the bloom of autumnal skies.

Ode to a Rose

You overromanticized bud,
You whose coat is drenched in vital blood,
Or the fluffy white tears of the sky,
Yours is an understated beauty,
Made public by the Valentines of the world.

E. L. Barnes

Ode to Self-Doubt

My confidant,
That voice inside my head,
I wrestle and kiss--
.
You keep me from making a fool of myself,
From embarrassing myself,
From trying new things that undoubtedly
Scare me.
You're the reason my room is always a mess
As I scour my closet for the perfect
outfit.
You're the reasons I'm close friends
with spell check, Grammarly, and autocorrect.
You're the reason I pick up that donut...
Glance down at my hips,
And put it back on the plate.
No one knows me better than you.
You're that overprotective grandmother walking
beside me,
Holding my hand,
Waiting for me to fall so you can pick me
Back up again.

A week in the life of a 23-year-old college student –

.
.
.
.
.
.
.
.
.
.
.

(2/10/21)
Afternoon, 2 PM
Skipped my class
Because periods...
Who needs them?
I'm not a baby factory.
Give me some chocolate
And tell the world to shut up.
Afternoon, 4:15 PM
In a meeting for
House Arrest
When I get a Facetime call
From A.K.
Needless to say,
I think he misses me.
Evening, 6 PM

A productive day,
I'm happy to say,
Now in my bed,
I'm delighted to lay,
And close my eyes to sleep.
Good night.
(2/11/21)
Mid-Morning, 11:20 AM
Yoga time
I inhale,
And exhale.
In and out.
Sun salutations and vinyasa flow.
Namaste.
Noon, 12 PM
While the house is being cleaned
I make a nest
In my Daddy's office.
There the words flow
And the first chapter is finished.
Praise the Lord.
Evening, 6 PM
As the hair & makeup designer for
House Arrest
I have to give tutorials
On how to look old.
Kill me now.
(2/12/21)
Morning, 9:30 AM
The Sun greets me with
The promise of a brand new day.

I don't dread the morning
Anymore.
I rise to the challenge of pursuing joy.

Afternoon, 2:46 PM
Running errands w/Mom
Bed, Bath & Beyond
For coffee.
BJ's for face wipes, crab meat, and pears.
Pistachio Latte at my favorite place—B&N.
Evening, 9 PM
Working on
A Light in the Darkness
Edited through the second
Chapter.
Making progress.
(2/13/21)
Morning, 4:30 AM
The unholy hour
Stretches before me.
Up before the Sun can
Rub its eyes.
Guess I better get a start
On the day.

Afternoon, 12:46 PM
Two cups of coffee later
And I'm asking for another one.
My fix, my fix,
"Can we get Starbucks?"
I went for the Crème Brulee

And don't regret it.
Evening, 8:40 PM
It's barely 9
Time for another
Love-dovey Hallmark Movie
Based on Jane Austen.
I can't keep my eyes open
Anymore.
It's been 16 hours.
(2/14/21)
Morning, 8 AM
Feeling so much
Better today.
Got at least ten hours
And my best is 9.
Ready to face the day
With my TickTick by my side.

Mid-Morning, 11 AM
Valentine's Day date with my
Daddy.
Getting breakfast while I'm
Decked out in hearts
And my leather suede boots.
#breakfastbuddies
Afternoon, 4:35 PM
Mad dash through Target
For cards, beauty packages, and gift cards.
My first day back to E.O. Bull
Since last March.
I finally feel

Like a good dancer.
(2/15/21)
Early Morning, 5:15 AM
It's early and I have to go pee.
I shouldn't have drank
All that water.
But I was thirsty.
And the water bottle called to me
Assuring me I made the right choice.
Early Morning 6:25 AM
Dear God,
Thank You for a great Valentine's Day—
One for the books.
I don't want to read this play and I'm sorry
Please let me get into the cabaret.
Thanks.
Still Early Morning, 6:57 AM
I finished the play.
The Nether.
There. It's done.
I am confusion.
What on earth is happening?
Why wasn't I warned…
.
.
.
.
.
.
.
.

.
.
.
.
(2/16/21)
Early Morning, 2 AM
Judy Corry
Writes great fiction.
I feel like I'm back in high school.
Crushes, and sports, and classes,
Makes me wish things were different—
That I wasn't stuck here.
Mid-Morning, 10 AM
Semi-regretting staying up late
That was the longest book of my life
But I identify with Eliana.
The heart can only take so much before it
Bursts.
Afternoon, 4:45 PM
So my Mom's getting a wig today.
Who said bone cancer has the upper hand?
My Mom would look great bald, gray, or with her
Raven black hair.
She says her hair was her one beauty,
But God sees the heart even while He counts the hairs.

ADC

Pushing and shoving,
Unkind words and girlish screams:
First week of day camp.

E. L. Barnes

Memos

Pulling up notes app
On my phone where it's quiet;
Pocket poetry.

Houseguests

I had my first houseguest when I was six. Her name was Obsessive-Compulsive Disorder, "OCD" for short. To be honest, though, I think she'd been living with me long before that. I just noticed her around that time.

The six-year-old version of me was dripping with sweat. I had just finished cleaning up my entire room and the intense amount of effort I'd put into the task had me huffing and puffing. My mouth was dry, my arms were tired. The only thing left to fix was the bed; I had to make my bed. I mean, what was the point of cleaning my room if my bed wasn't made?

Little arms pumping back and forth, I wrestled the pale green and purple butterfly comforter into place. One by one, I leaned the pillows against the butter-yellow headboard. Then, it happened, or rather, *she* happened.

You see, there was this one particular, little throw pillow that didn't want to sit exactly upright, and every time I went to stand at the foot of the bed to admire my work, OCD would come up behind me and whisper in my ear.

"Uh-uh-uh, girlie. You're not finished yet. Not until that pillow is perfect."

So, I tried to fix it. And tried. And tried. Five times went by, then ten. Tears stung my eyes as I pulled and pinched and tugged at that cursed pillow.

"Why does it have to be perfect?" I screamed inside the confines of my head, the pillow clutched in my tiny hands. I chucked the offensive clump of artificial fluff across the room.

"Because," OCD replied, as if the answer were obvious and completely rational, *"it just has to be."*

Her logic didn't seem sound to me but for some reason, I couldn't help myself. The desire to restore order was too strong. Sure, I didn't *want* to fix the pillow. That thing could burn to high heaven for all I cared at that point. No, I didn't want to; I had to, I needed to, because OCD demanded it of me. She made me obsess over the false belief that everything in my world had to be perfect and then compelled me to run ragged trying to make everything perfect anytime it wasn't, which, as you can guess, was often. Very often.

Resigned, six-year-old me picked up the pillow and tried again. I had started cleaning my room around noon. It was dark outside when OCD finally gave me a thumbs-up. I haven't liked throw pillows since.

Shortly after OCD moved in, I was introduced to her younger sister. Her name was Anxiety. She told surprisingly scary stories for such a snotty-nosed kid. The ones that keep you up late into the night, the ones that send dizzying shocks of terror through your heart when you least expect it, the ones that make you dry-heave at daddy-daughter camping trips during story time, and check under your bed, behind your bedroom door, and every corner of your closet twice. As always, Anxiety's stories were based on truth, which made them all the harder to shake. One occasion comes to mind with frightening clarity.

Seven-year-old me was sleeping over at my best friend's house. It was the very first time I had ever slept over at anyone's house before, and so far, we'd been having a great time. Go Fish, Hide-n-Seek, dress-up, make-believe; we played it all. About half an hour before bed, my friend's parents decided to turn on the news. Immediately, the words "BREAKING NEWS" flashed onto the screen. The headline: "LOCAL GRANDMA BEATEN TO DEATH WITH A FRYING PAN BY HER GRANDSON". Oh, my, did Anxiety like that. So did her sister.

The fear that coursed through my veins as I watched the footage of the policeman barging through the doors of that poor woman's house and examining her battered, lifeless body at the bottom of her stairs pumped with a fiery intensity that was unmatched. It stole my breath, knocked me on my knees, and had me sob-shouting at my best friend's parents to turn the TV off, but they wouldn't.

"It's just a story." They told me as they continued to watch the following explanation of how the grandmother was murdered by her own flesh and blood simply because he needed some money. They watched as if such an event were to be studied rather than mourned and feared, which scared me even more.

"If it's just a story, then why is it on the news? It happened, right?"

"Well, yes. But far away from here." I wasn't convinced. The damage had already been done. Anxiety had latched onto a story, and OCD was screening it through the lenses of my eyeballs on a constant loop. "Besides, the young man's already been caught, so there's nothing to worry about."

"Nothing to worry about?", Anxiety snickered in my ear.

"Shut up. Just shut up. I don't want to hear it."

She didn't listen. *"Try this one on for size: 'LOCAL TEXAS GIRL MURDERED WITH A FRYING PAN WHILE STAYING THE NIGHT AT HER FRIEND'S HOUSE'."*

"I said shut up! I don't want to hear it!"

"Ooh, I like it! I think it should be on a 24/7 newscast kind of thing. Ya know, 'LOCAL TEXAS GIRL MURDERED WITH A FRYING PAN WHILE STAYING THE NIGHT AT HER FRIEND'S HOUSE.'"

"Good idea!"

"Cut it out!"

" 'LOCAL TEXAS GIRL MURDERED WITH A FRYING PAN WHILE STAYING THE NIGHT'…"

"STOP IT!"

" 'LOCAL TEXAS GIRL MURDERED WITH A FRYING PAN'..."

"Please...stop."

" 'LOCAL TEXAS GIRL MURDERED'... 'TEXAS GIRL MURDERED'... 'GIRL MURDERED'... 'MURDERED'...MURDERED."

I called my mom shortly after that.

"I don't understand why you can't just get over it." My best friend said, watching me roll up my sleeping bag and pack away my toys.

"I wish I could." *But they won't let me.*

A few minutes later, my Dad showed up. It was 2 am and God bless him, he showed up. Not that being home made going to sleep any easier. Nothing was ever easy with my two houseguests.

I thought for sure they'd leave. Eventually. Stupid, naive, idealistic me. They stayed. And the longer they stayed, the angrier I became, at everyone. My mom, my dad, my younger brother, my friends, me. I'd lash out at the most unremarkable things in tantrums possessing a fury unbeknownst to man, only to be stopped when my little body finally gave out and fell asleep. Anger was my constant companion during those days.

I just want them out of my head, I'd tell myself again and again as if repeating my wish would make it come true. That seemed to work for OCD whenever she wanted to get me to do something, so why couldn't I use that same type of obsessive-compulsive-wishful thinking on myself? Why, if I was so miserable, couldn't I kick my unwanted houseguests out of my brain? Make them vacate the premises?

The answer was simple: I didn't have the power to kick them out. Authority, yes. It was my house, my head, after all, but clearly, that didn't matter to OCD and Anxiety. No, kicking those two pests out required power, power I didn't have, at that time, or any time.

So, I found someone who could kick them out, a guy with all the power. His name was Jesus.

I'd heard His Name mentioned a couple of times around church, even heard my Mom and Dad talking to him, and from what I gathered, He seemed like an all-around, decent guy; very forgiving, very loving. That was all well and good, but I needed an exterminator, not a new landlord. Turns out, I needed both.

"For <u>all</u> have sinned and fallen short of the glory of God...Come to me, all you who are weary...and I will give you rest..."

Rest? What *was* "rest"? It was a foreign concept to my seven-year-old psyche, but I wanted it. I wanted it more than anything. I mean, this Jesus-guy offered a pretty good deal: not only would He get rid of my unwanted "pest guests", but He also promised to fix up my house, inside and out, until it looked as good as new; until *I* was good as new. The real icing on the cake? The eternal lease He gave me on my place, completely and absolutely rent-free. All I had to do was turn over the keys of my house, my mind, my heart, my everything to Him. All I had to do was believe.

"There's really nothing else I have to do?" my little self asked in the quiet of my head, as I folded my hands and bowed my head for the first time. I could feel Jesus smile. He shook his head.

"Then stay as long as you like."

Another soft smile. *"I'll stay as long as you'll have Me. I only ask that you take care of Faith and Hope here."* Faith was a sprouting in a brown, clay pot. Hope a lily-white infant. *"They're gonna need someone to look after them."*

"I think I can do that."

"Don't worry," Jesus said, *"Joy will help you."*

And she did. Out of all of us, she was the one who liked kids the most. I say all of us because Joy was the first in a long line of new houseguests that took up residence in my home (after Rest, that is). Except this time, I didn't mind. This time, I welcomed them in.

Eventually, Joy brought Peace, who helped sing Hope to sleep. Then came Truth (the Bible-lover who told it like it was) and Forgiveness, or "Anti-OCD" as I sometimes liked to call her. Yes sirree, those two were great. I mean, the moment Jesus took possession of my house, Truth and Forgiveness swooped in with large, plastic garbage bags and started throwing all OCD, Anxiety, and even Anger's stuff out. Their lies, their scary stories, their impossible expectations, all out the front door and onto the curb with the trash, where that mental garbage belonged. It was amazing to see and even better to experience.

And Jesus. Oh, that Jesus. He really knows how to sweep a girl off her feet. Where there were accusations of false guilt and threats of violence and terror echoing up and down the corridors of my mind there were now rooms filled with His voice, serenading me lovingly as he twirled me around in the living room. Who wouldn't fall for a guy like that? At seven years old, I was in love with my landLord-Exterminator: hook, line, and sinker.

For years my house was like this, full of laughter, happy, and carefree. Of course, there were times when OCD would drop by unannounced, with her bratty sister in tow. It was funny. I didn't even have to answer the door. In a flash, Jesus was there to promptly show them out.

"You have no place here," He'd say simply, though there was an unwavering hint of steel in His voice every time they came a-knockin', *"and this is not your house."*

High school, I believe, is when my metaphysical paradise fell apart. In the span of my junior year, I lost my grandfather, the long-standing romance I had with my middle-school crush fizzled and some of my friendships burst into flames, thanks to the twins, Rumor, and Gossip. Yep. That kicked off my senior year. Day after day, for months, Pain would slap me across the face. Betrayal would punch me in the gut. Denial, well, he'd patch me up and tell me I was imagining things.

To their credit, Joy and Peace tried to stick it out, but I'll admit, I was a bit hard on them. They were the first ones to leave; Rest went out the window. It was then that Anger made a reappearance. With Pain came Despair and with Betrayal came Bitterness. Depression settled in shortly afterward. He was the biggest bully of them all. The floodgates really blew open once he arrived. Insecurity, Self-loathing, Doubt, Suspicion, Insomnia--- yea, they all moved in before my high school graduation. I begrudgingly confess, that this diverted my attention away from Faith, who withered down to a nub. Hope was nowhere to be found.

Somehow, around the fall of 2016, word got around (again, I blame Rumor and Gossip), and to no one's surprise but my own, OCD was back with her sister, Anxiety. Man, how that snotty-nosed brat had grown. She was taller than me and at times, smarter. She hit it off with Depression right away. Together, they liked to whisper lies in my ear about how "easy" and "noble" my life would be if I would just simply put an end to it, once and for all. I didn't think it possible, but the two of them actually managed to kick Truth and Forgiveness out. It was a shame because I really liked them.

I guess OCD felt lonely once her kid sister got a boyfriend because it was around that same time that she got Vicious Cycle, a narcissistic parrot with a mouth as foul as fowl, who'd pick up on any and every curse word, perverse idea, or unsettling thought she heard with a vengeance. It was the *"24/7 Frying Pan Newscast"* all over again, except with a squawking bird as the news anchor (which is fitting I suppose...).

The noise was unbearable. March of my sophomore year in college, Nervous Breakdown paid me a visit.

It was a cool spring evening when I began screaming at my mother at the top of my lungs in the middle of our front yard, decked out in a grease-stained hoodie and a week-old pair of sweatpants. The day before, she and I had gotten into a fight. You know the kind of fight I'm talking about the-why-can't-you-just-make-your-brother-a-chicken-sandwich-when-he-asks-you-to-even-though-he's-perfectly-capable-of-making-it-himself kind of fight? Anyway, my mom ended up making the sandwich, which made her less than happy, and I thought her reaction was unwarranted. Clearly, the breakdown wasn't about the chicken sandwich because what I ended up saying was:

> "I don't want to do this anymore! I can't do this anymore."

> "What can't you do?"

I stared at her. "Live. I can't live anymore. I don't want to live anymore."

"Why don't you want to live anymore?" my mother asked, tears welling in her eyes. Her voice was still.

"Because I'm a failure."

"You're not a fail---"

"I'm a failure! I fail at everything! I fail at being a good student, I fail at being a writer, I fail at being a sister, I fail at being a daughter, I fail at life! I fail at everything, Mommy." I sucked in a chest-rattling breath. Wiped at the streaks on my face with the back of my sleeve. Sighed. "And I'm just so tired of it. I'm tired, Mommy. I'm tired of failing." *I'm tired of hearing these voices in my head. I'm tired of not being able to sleep. I'm tired of living in a full house. I'm tired of...*

My mother looked at me, her lip trembling. "Does that seem normal to you? That you want to end your life because you think you're a failure? Does that *sound* normal to you?" *No. It doesn't.* "Is that how Jesus would want you to think of yourself? As a failure?" *No. He wouldn't.*

A knot coiled inside my gut at the frightening realization that in the midst of all the influx of unwanted houseguests, the One person Who wasn't supposed to ever be a houseguest was no longer living in my house. Somehow, somewhere along the lines of my suffering,

I'd kicked Jesus out and sealed myself inside the walls of an abusive home.

That's the great thing about Jesus, though. No matter how many times you kick Him out, He never gets mad, never makes you feel guilty. He just waits. And waits. He waits until you're clawing at the door of your house, desperate for an escape. He waits until You need a faithful landLord, a kick-butt Exterminator, or a loving Savior.

I can still remember what He said to me, that day I lost it on the front lawn over a chicken sandwich.

"You know I can get rid of them, right?"

"Yeah, I know...I guess I forgot that."

"Yes, you did, but it's all right. I'm here now."

"...Thanks."

"What is it?

"I want them <u>all</u> gone. Can You do that?"

"Oh, honey. Your war has already been won."

Today, I'm discovering that while Jesus may have won the war, every day is a battle I must face, but I do not face it alone. I know that now. Every day I must decide whether I'm willing to let Jesus inside my house, and every day I do make that choice, He kicks another houseguest out and moves another friend back in. Sometimes this occurs as a supernatural thing, but more often than not, it happens as a result of something as physical and tangible as going to talk with a counselor, discussing possible medical treatments with my doctor, becoming aware of my unique body chemistry, journaling, learning healthier ways to relieve stress, etc. Of course, I attribute this burgeoning relationship with Health to Jesus. I attribute everything good to Jesus.

He is my Savior, my landLord, my Healer, my Exterminator, and He cleans house for me every single day. Now, let me ask you this:

How clean is *your* house?

E. L. Barnes

Part III

The Scary Thing

I think the scariest thing is not knowing if You can get through.
What if my heart is impenetrable?
I can't tell if it's stony, lukewarm and indifferent, callous and cold, or just plain cruel.
Or if it's a lethal combination of all of the above.
I can't tell if it's been fortified by walls, barbed wire, a moat, or if it's in a dank dungeon, under lock and key.
If so, where is the key? Because it's sure as heaven not with me.
If I had it, I would give it to You.
But I can't find it,
And yea...I think *that's* the scariest thing of all.

#2020

I'm fighting over toilet paper in a masked crowd of angry shoppers while crying over all the voices inside my head that whisper "you're alone now, give up." Passing by the kitchen after closing the front door and squirting sanitizer on my hands (from Bath & Body Works of course) and shopping for the cutest mask that will hopefully last past this "new normal". I'm shut away for days upon days and weeks upon weeks and months upon months in the one word I've grown to hate:

Quarantine.

I'm forced to go to classes that don't interest me anymore because they took out the human interaction element. Who would've thought *I* would want to hang out with people...in *person*? And now there's another word I hate:

Zoom.

And I'm sorry...but what the heck is with all the tOiLeT pApEr???

Vulnerable

To push past doubt,
To push past fear,
To push past the overwhelming desire--
To be complacent.
That is a risk--
That reaps the sweetest reward.

E. L. Barnes

Heart Cry

You tug on the strings of my heart,
Like your servant plucks out the delicate melody of the harp.
You invite me into Your g o l d e n place;
I'll never be the same.
My heart thirsts for your lovingkindness,
The peace You bring
By the sound of Your voice.
I have heard You call to me in the dead of night,
In the quiet moments of a hectic day.
My heart has heard you say, "Come and talk with me."
And my heart responds, "Lord, I am coming."

It's hard to talk to yourself about being afraid--
But even when my feelings overwhelm me--
My heart will remain confident.
My heart will be u n b r e a k a b l e.
It will bend and it will quiver,
But it will *not* break.
My body may break
And my soul may be trampled,
But this I say for certain:
He is the strength of my heart--
He is mine
Forever.

Count Your Blessings

(*White Christmas,* December 2022.)

Count your blessings...
What does that mean
Exactly?
.

Does it mean that we shrug off pain and loss in favor of joking around?
.

Does it mean that we laugh out loud when all we want to do is cry inside?
.

Does it mean that we put on an act, even when we're off the stage?
.

No--
It means we're brave enough to be real,
brave enough to recognize that everything is
not fine,
that we are not fine and
that's ok

Counting our blessings means
being thankful that things aren't worse
(because they could always be worse) and
acknowledging all the right things in our lives
Because there are *so* many right things...
.

A family I choose,

but a family that chose me first.

.

Friends that lift you up and hold you when
you fall down on the job

.

Loved ones you are excited to just say hello to first thing
on a Friday night,
that you genuinely feel blessed by
because you got to sit down and talk to them for a while

.

Pumping Christmas music through the speakers
that bring the holidays to life for "ten glorious minutes"

.

People who sing songs with you and treasure you and
respect you--

.

.

.

So.
Many.
Right things.

And I truly believe, that when we count our blessings
instead of sheep, if we choose to be active in capturing
our thoughts instead of passively letting them
overwhelm us--

Well then,
eventually
we will discover that we might
actually

finally
be
ok.

And that is just another blessing.
Another wonderfully, imperfectly perfect
Right thing.

E. L. Barnes

Life in Living Colors

Periwinkle skies,
Seas of lavender moon blooms,
Translucent haven.

Peel back the wrapping
Of tin foil and silly string;
Joke's on you, April Fools'.

Crest of the ocean
Gem of the manicured lawn;
Foam and grass trimmings.

Waves of yeasty grain
Sweeping over the fields of gold
Spinning yarns of lore.

Pomegranate drinks,
With those tiny umbrellas.
Oxblood and crimson.

Pumpkin spice lattes,
Smells of musty autumn winds,
Orange-tinted eyes.

Up in Flames

There's a stirring in the air
that skates across my skin.
There's the burnt smell of toast
that singes the insides of my nostrils.
There's a sizzling crack on the buffeting wind
that shatters my heart; my place.
My home.
There's a corpse of a wooden sanctuary before me,
that sears the edges of my self-control.
My place; my home.
There's metal in my mouth
from biting my lip
so hard.
My life.
My place.
My home.
Gone.
.
.
.

Up in flames.

E. L. Barnes

Disguise

When I look into your eyes,
You disguise falls aways and I can see you clearly.
Just look into my eyes--
Into my eyes...

Just *look*.

Something New

So change my heart,
And turn it into something new;

Make me willing to be made willing
To love You.

E. L. Barnes

Dangerous Melody

Broken needles
and paper cuts.
Dark alleys
and late-night parking lots.
Mystery brownies
and gas station shrimp tacos.
(Ew.)
Infected scabs
and bleeding blisters,
strangers and stranger men,
white vans and "can I walk you home?"
That last hit…
Just a little more.
To feel,
To breathe,
That's the real danger.
The need to die to live.
A dangerous melody.

Does it Ever Occur to You?

Does it ever occur to you that what you do—
hurts me?
Does it ever occur to you that when you say that—
it stings?
Does it ever occur to you that when you act that way—
you belittle me,
demean me,
humiliate and alienate me?
No—
I guess not.
Then again,
It never occurs to me that
you're going through your own stuff.
But it's no excuse.
Does it ever occur to you that saying
"I'm sorry" goes a long way?
No?
I guess not.

E. L. Barnes

dancing barefoot in the grass with You

I find myself here quite often.
It doesn't many how many years,
How much I think I've grown.
I'm here—
Again.
Where?
It's a place I've known from birth.
A place I will go when I die.
There's no pain, no suffering, no tears.
And yet,
I'm afraid.
I don't want to leave here.
A few years go by,
And I find myself here.
The beginning of everything.
A new hallelujah.
Mercies new every morning.
The sun rises
And all is well.

The Recipe of a Faithful Servant

Serving as God's child
Is as simple as breathing:
Start with a hand,
Add a heart,
Supply the will,
Dedicate the mind,
And mix in some soul.
~
All that flows,
Flows from Him.

E. L. Barnes

That's the Tea

Let me tell you about my favorite mug: it's an unusual
shape. Sort of a square with rounded edges that
gets smaller toward the lip. I got it from Five Below.
It's powder pink with white cursive letters that say,
"That's the Tea." I love it because I use it for coffee
OR tea and whenever I look at it, I'm immediately
enveloped by a feeling of warmth, comfort, and peace.
I feel like I can really pour out my heart to whoever
may be listening while I sip my steaming beverage.
It encourages me to be real, honest; raw. I can say
anything, either to myself or to a trusted loved one.
And that's the tea. ;)

Melt Away

Around me there's so many things I,
don't wanna face, don't wanna feel--
I can't find my way out.

I'm lost in a sea of distractions...
I'm stuck with my head up in the clouds.

So melt away--
All the things that keep me from knowing You.
And melt my heart, God--

So I can follow after You.

E. L. Barnes

Storm

If wishes fell like rain,
Then certainly I am a storm.
My mind is blurring
With dreams I've never dreamed before.
I'm buzzing,
Images and sensations and feelings
All entirely foreign to me---
And yet, I want more.
So I wish and I wish and I wish
Not upon a star or clover,
Not upon a dandelion,
But upon the rain;
Upon that glorious storm.

Ode to Evie

Tiny, little kitty cat.
Throwing a fit over birds.
A furry protector.

Love at First Sight

There is a stirring,
Butterflies awaken now---
Within my stomach.

When I Get There

There is something strange,
About accomplishing goals;
What do I do now?

E. L. Barnes

A Love Letter to Close

Dear God,

You know. It's been hard for me to pray, truly pray and talk openly/honestly with You for years. It's been hard to bring things to You and be real. I don't know why, but I know You haven't changed.

You never change.

But it would seem I have.

Your love is still the same--Your forgiveness is still there. Can I say the same?

Your thoughts are always around me--Are my thoughts always around You?

I forget and I hate how I forget You.

I've abandoned my house and I saw I want nothing more than to come back, but my actions don't line up. What will it take to bring me back?

And am I willing to die to my own desires so that I can rise in glory with You?

I do love You, Lord.
In Christ's Name, I pray. I ask for help, for the courage to acknowledge Your love, and the willingness to be made complete in Your Presence.

Amen.

(until the next volume)

Like this book?

Leave a review!

Want to keep up to date with E. L. Barnes?

Connect with the author on Facebook or Instagram!

www.ingramcontent.com/pod-product-compliance
Lightning Source LLC
Chambersburg PA
CBHW030447220526
45464CB00006B/2444